D1006681

Let's Go Outside

STICKS AND STONES –
NATURE ADVENTURES, GAMES
AND PROJECTS FOR KIDS

Let's Go
Outside

STICKS AND STONES –
NATURE ADVENTURES, GAMES
AND PROJECTS FOR KIDS

Steph Scott
And
Katie Akers

BATSFORD

Dedication

To Ben and Sophie.
You rock ... I'm so lucky.
S.S.

To Ma.
K.A.

First published in the United Kingdom in 2015
by Batsford, an imprint of
Pavilion Books Company Limited
1 Gower Street
London WC1E 6HD
www.pavilionbooks.com

ISBN 9781849942768

A CIP catalogue record for this book is available
from the British Library.

20 19 18 17 16 15
10 9 8 7 6 5 4 3 2 1

Reproduction by Rival Colour Ltd, UK
Printed and bound by 1010 Printing International
   Ltd, China

This book can be ordered direct from
the publisher at the website:
www.pavilionbooks.com
or try your local bookshop.

Distributed in the United States and Canada by
Sterling Publishing Co., Inc.
1166 Avenue of the Americas, 17th Floor,
New York, NY 10036

Contents

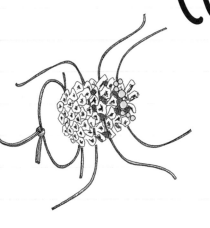

Foreword 8

INTRODUCTION 10
Let's Go Outside 12
The Out Pack 13
What's in the Out Pack? 14
How to Forage 15
How Does it All Work? 16
What is an Outpacker? 17
How to Remember Your Seasons 18

NATURE MAKES 20

THE OUT-PACK GAMES 64

OUT AND ABOUTS 98

SKILLS 126

So You're an Outpacker ... 140
Fun Stuff to See and Read 141
Index 142
Acknowledgements 144

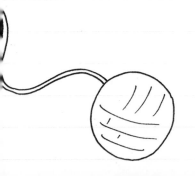

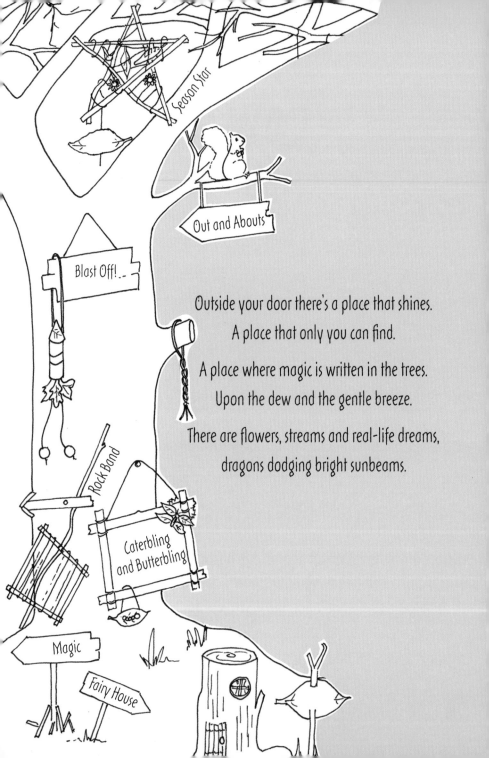

Season Star

Out and Abouts

Blast Off!

Rock Band

Caterbling
and Butterbling

Magic

Fairy House

Outside your door there's a place that shines.
A place that only you can find.

A place where magic is written in the trees.
Upon the dew and the gentle breeze.

There are flowers, streams and real-life dreams,
dragons dodging bright sunbeams.

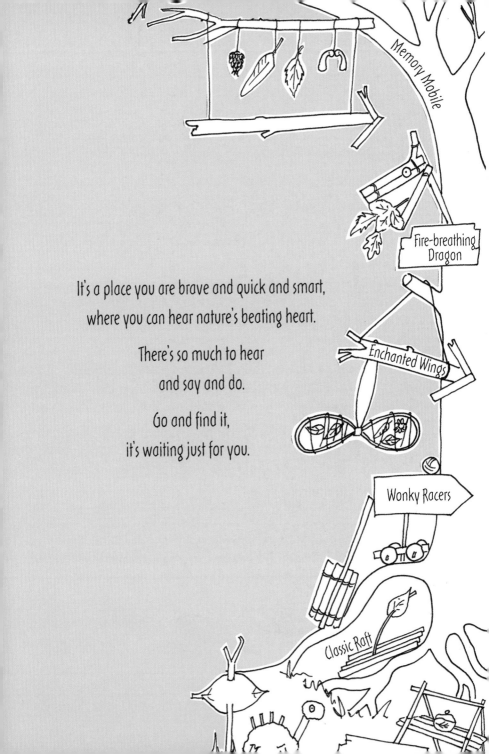

Memory Mobile

Fire-breathing Dragon

Enchanted Wings

It's a place you are brave and quick and smart,
where you can hear nature's beating heart.

There's so much to hear
and say and do.

Go and find it,
it's waiting just for you.

Wonky Racers

Classic Raft

Foreword

My earliest memory is watching flames in a little campfire in a stream-bed in North Yorkshire. It was the first time I remember paying proper attention to what was around me. Everywhere there was something exciting – an ant on its way home with food, a spider weaving. I remember feeling very safe, and very calm. I was with members of my family who were showing me how to enjoy being outside. They were giving me permission to love nature.

To take their first adventurous steps outside, children need persuasion to let go of the indoors, of addictive screens and toys. But there is a big obstacle to that first step: uncertainty about what to do, both for adults and children. We are increasingly used to dealing with manufactured things and we all find it hard to play in an undirected way with a stick or with leaves.

This lovely book by Steph and Katie is so important because it provides a path to help children to rediscover undirected play. Along the way, I rediscovered my permission to enjoy the outdoors.

Let's Go Outside contains a wonderful gift. Try the activities and children will start to rewrite and recreate the ideas, and then generate new and more wonderful games. It sows a creative seed and is helping to train up the next generation of wild things.

DAVID BOND

David Bond made the film *Project Wild Thing* and is director of The Wild Network, a group of organisations and individuals campaigning to get more children outside. Steph and Katie are members – join in at www.projectwildthing.com.

Introduction

Welcome to you all: children, parents, grandparents, uncles, aunts, teachers, forest-school leaders, childminders, and all flora and fauna everywhere. Whether you are already passionate about nature and the outdoors, or are just taking your first steps into the woods, you are very welcome. This book is written for you all.

Let's Go Outside

Let's Go Outside is a new kind of activity book for children aged 3–7 years. It is a book of original and simple outdoor activities, games, nature facts and woodland skills. It can fill a quick half hour in the backyard or a week-long camping trip out in the wilderness.

The Out Pack

The Out Pack is the other thing you need in order to make the magic happen. It is your child's own special backpack containing all the bits and pieces required to complete the activities, in addition to a few items that they can easily forage from nature. Your child's Out Pack is any bag that is comfy for them to wear and can hold everything they need. The Out Pack is the doorway to a childhood of outdoor adventures, bringing nature that bit closer to home. When your child has an Out Pack on his or her back, they're off screen, outdoors and breathing fresh air; they have everything they need to make anything they'd like out of this book.

What your child might choose to do today depends only on their mood, the season, the weather and how much outdoor space and time is available. Together you could make a pair of enchanted wings and spend an afternoon flying around a forest. You could create a games kit (see pages 68–69) and spend hours playing games from wobble catch to croquet. You could go on an Out and About and have fun learning the names of trees, bugs and clouds, or you could sit and learn some valuable woodland skills. As long as you know a stick from a stone and a pine cone from a leaf, you're ready for some adventures.

What's in the Out Pack?

All the items in the Out Pack are easy to find and cheap to buy. You may already have some of them at home. Be sure to keep it well stocked so you don't run out of any essentials while you're out and about. This is a list of what we keep in our Out Packs ...

- This book!
- Coloured pens
- Masking tape: you won't need anything thicker than 12mm wide
- Wool: you can get two balls of different colours, a multi-coloured ball or just a ball of your favourite colour
- Plastic-coated garden wire: you can buy this in a reel with a safe cutter from anywhere that sells garden supplies
- Elastic bands: flat elastic bands of many colours are useful
- Paperclips
- Ball of string
- Wooden beads: big and small, bumpy and smooth
- Child-friendly scissors: they must be able to cut string

A Small Note

Let's Go Outside and the Out Pack are intended for interactive adventures outdoors. Children will need your help and supervision with many parts of the creative process. We recommend that when the Out Pack is open, there is an adult nearby to lend a hand. When your child's Out Pack is at home and not being played with, it is best placed in a high spot out of their reach. There are items in there that children need a helping hand with and we're sure that you'd rather not wind that ball of string up again and again and again!

How to Forage

Don't worry if you don't know what some of the trees and plants that you're foraging for look like. In our Out and Abouts chapter (see page 98) we've created some fun ways to identify and remember the flora and fauna that you will need to complete all the activities in this book.

Foraging is a wonderful skill that will help your child with every part of their Out Pack experience. It is basically about searching and finding. Kids love to pick up bits and pieces from nature so they're likely to be very accomplished foragers already. In a nutshell, it's about helping your child to search for and find whatever they might be looking for, and it's especially about helping them to know what is okay to take from nature. It's about gathering this up and discovering, not only how incredible all these treasures are, but also the wonderful things that we can make with them.

Foraging is a long walk for the perfect stick; it is finding the sycamore pod that flies best; and knowing when you've found a weeping willow and how it can help you make a million and one things.

Most of the creations in *Let's Go Outside* can be made with bits and pieces from nature that can be found on the ground. You will, however, also find that there are a handful of creations that require foraging items from nature that are still living. These may be a few wild flowers from a lawn or meadow, a short stick of elder wood, a green leaf from a luscious hedge or a willow shoot.

We have specifically chosen trees and plants that are known to be robust, fast growers that are abundant throughout the year. They are trees and plants that like to be pruned and can cope with us carefully taking small bits from them. Having said that, if you find a willow tree that is looking a bit lacklustre, perhaps leave him until he appears a bit livelier.

How does it all work?

Let's Go Outside and your Out Pack are designed for each other. The book has the ideas and the pack delivers the means to achieving them. All you need to do is decide what you are going to do today, go foraging for the bits that you need from nature, take out whatever is required from your Out Pack and follow the instructions. The rest is down to your imagination.

What is an Outpacker?

Outpackers are amazing. They know all about nature and how to take care of it. They also know how to take care of themselves outdoors – how to stay warm, dry and safe. Use these rhymes and raps to help you as you take your first steps to becoming an Outpacker ...

If it's made by nature it can stay, if it's from the Out Pack take it away.

Berries, berries never pick
They can make you super sick.

Snow, wind, rain or shine
Weather changes all the time
Keep a mac inside your pack
And something spare to warm your back.

Sticks in faces are no good
Keep it down like you know you should
Watch it, watch it, watch it ...

My stick is longer than my arm
If I wave it around it will do harm
Drag it, drag it, drag it ...

Fungi, fungi never touch
They will hurt you very much.

Keep adventures right on track
Don't get caught without a snack.

How to Remember Your Seasons

It can be a bit tricky to remember the seasons, coming and going and going and coming all the time, and as we talk about them a lot in this book, we've made up a little rhyme to help you remember them. You can sing it to the tune of the nursery rhyme 'Twinkle, Twinkle, Little Star', or you can say it as a rap, or you can learn it just as it is. It goes like this:

Winter feels so very cold
In spring the little buds unfold
Summer's green all down the lane
Autumn all comes down again
Seasons come and then they go ...
nature's dazzling magic show!

So ...

Let's go outside and celebrate nature. From the smallest backyard to the largest wilderness. Let's go outside, wherever you may be.

Let's go outside and discover the magic; plants, animals, seasons and weather. Let's marvel at it all.

Let's go outside and imagine – kids delight in their little piece of crafted nature that can take them to the moon and back.

Let's go outside with the Out Pack ...

Coat, boots, Out Pack and go!

Nature Makes

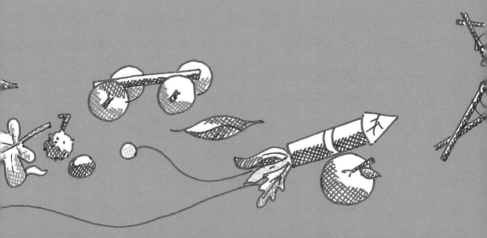

A 'nature make' is just as it sounds – ...
it is something you make out of nature.

From fallen sticks and leaves, wild flowers and feathers, a nature make can open the door to a whole world of imagination. It can take you across the ocean chasing rainbows, on a flight through an enchanted forest, zooming around a racing track, or blasting into space. It can make you the proud owner of your own mud pie and sweet shop, the lead singer of a rock band, or take you on an adventure into the secret world of puddles. Nature makes are about finding and creating, but most of all they are about the magic that happens after you've made something fabulous out of wonderful nature.

Thankfully nature is extremely kind to us Outpackers. It's a bit like a really generous friend who can't stop buying presents for us all. Every year it makes a whole feast of treats for us to eat, to build and create with, and to marvel at. Each little piece is perfectly made, as if the world's most incredible sculptor had spent a lifetime creating it. Nature rocks!

So I wonder what you can you find in nature? I bet you can spot even a little bit, not very far from your front door. Go on, search and forage and see what treats you can find.

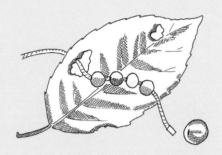

Do you know what you'd like to make today? If you can't decide then have a look at the world around you – nature will give you plenty of clues. Which season is it? In summer you might find a luscious willow tree that you can cut a stem from to make a pair of enchanted wings (see page 24). In autumn you might find fallen apples to make a wonky racer (see page 38). In winter there will be plenty of sticks for you to make a fire-breathing dragon from (see page 48), and spring might bring freshly fallen blossom to decorate your season star (see page 42).

Whatever you decide to make, you shouldn't have to go far to find the bits and pieces that you need from nature. If you're going to the park, for a walk in the woods, or even hanging out in your own backyard, there are lots of things that you can create. Gather together your nature treasures with the bits you need from your Out Pack and ask mum or dad to help you follow the instructions. And wherever we suggest a length of string, wool or a stick, we mean your arm or finger length, not your mum's or dad's.

Remember, our instructions are only a guide to get you going. Let your imagination take you wherever you'd like to go.

Enchanted Wings

There are magical places here and there that you can only get to if you have a pair of enchanted wings. Decorated with soft feathers, wild flowers, leaves, beads and more, you will be able to glide with dragons, dodge the blossom and chase the ladybirds.

COLLECT TOGETHER

From nature:
2-arm's length of willow, snapped at its join
Leaves
Wild flowers
Feathers

From the Out Pack:
Scissors
Masking tape
String
Wool
Garden wire
Beads

HOW TO MAKE IT:

1. Bend the willow into a bow shape to make the wings (if it snaps don't worry, you can have triangular wings) and secure with masking tape in the centre.

2. Cut a two-arm's length of wool.

3. Tie the wool to the willow at one end of the wings.

4. With the wool, create a zig-zag effect by winding the wool over and under the willow frame. As you go, thread beads on to the wool for decoration. Keep going until both of the wings are decorated.

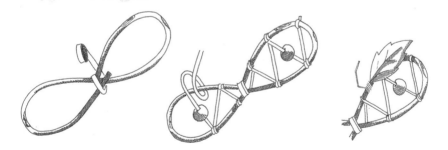

5. Cut enough hand-length pieces of wire for you to attach your chosen foragings – feathers, leaves and wild flowers. Wind the wire round and round your foragings to attach them to the wings.

6. Cut a two-arm's length of string, and tie the middle of the string over the masking tape in the centre of the wings. Put your wings on by taking the string over your shoulders, under your arms and tying around your back.

Caterbling and Butterbling

Have you ever heard a rap about some outdoor bling?
Well don't you fear, let me tell you something,
This ain't about getting dressed up for the ball,
Just really cool bling looking great on you all ...

Caterbling

COLLECT TOGETHER

From nature:

A tough leaf with at least two holes where
it's been munched by a hungry caterpillar

From the Out Pack:

Wool

Beads

Masking tape

Scissors

Coloured pens

HOW TO MAKE IT

1. Cut a two-arm's length of wool.

2. Cut a finger thickness of masking tape and wrap it around one end of the piece of wool. This is the working end.

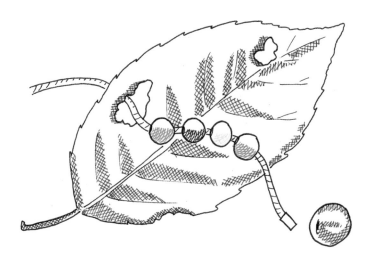

3. Thread the working end of the wool through the first hole in the leaf, from the back of the leaf to the front.

4. Create your caterpillar by threading on enough beads to span the two holes. You can finish with a larger bead for the head.

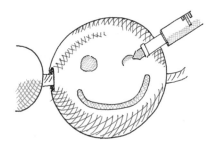

5. Thread the wool through the second hole in the leaf.

6. Tie it loosely around your neck. You might want to draw a little face on the head of your caterpillar so he can carry on munching!

Butterbling

COLLECT TOGETHER

From nature:

Four leaves

Two antennae; you can use flowers
or seed heads with stalks for these

From the Out Pack:

Paperclip

Garden wire

Masking tape

Bead

Wool

HOW TO MAKE IT

1. Make a bracelet by plaiting wool
(see skills section, page 138) and
thread a bead onto the bracelet.

2. Take your four leaves and secure
them into a butterfly shape with
a paperclip.

3. Cut a hand length of garden wire. Thread it up through the bottom of the paperclip, over the leaves and back through the top. Then thread it through the bead and secure with a pinch and twist. This attaches your butterfly to your bracelet.

4. Use a finger length of masking tape to stick your antennae to the top of the paper clip. Draw a face onto the masking tape.

5. Tie the wool to your wrist and your butterbling is ready to fly.

The Classic Raft

Be sure you know how to make a raft. You see there are giant waves at times, and sparkling rainbows and sunsets that need chasing. At other times there are raging rapids and cunning pirates who make you walk the plank. If I were you, I'd get some sticks and have a play, make a raft ... and sail away.

HOW TO MAKE IT

1. First cut a piece of string of about two arm lengths.

2. Tie a fish-on-a-dish knot (clove hitch) on to the end of one of your finger sticks (see skills section, page 130).

3. Take all of your finger sticks and line them up next to each other, creating the base of the raft.

4. Weave your string under and over each of the sticks in turn, fastening the sticks together.

5. Tighten the string in between the sticks by winding the tail end of the string around each of the three joints (this is called lashing – see skills section, page 132).

6. Repeat steps 1–5 at the other end of the raft.

7. Push your leaf over the top of your thin stick. Push and wiggle it into the middle string joint at one end of the raft to create the sail and mast of your raft.

8. Now look the whole way across the ocean, all the way to the horizon. There's the most colourful rainbow that needs chasing – go on, go catch it! But watch out for pirates ...

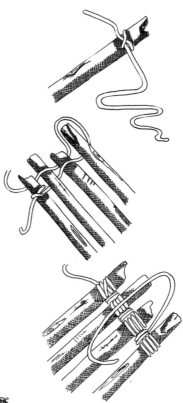

31

Memory Mobile

As one of the world's greatest adventurers, it is your job to have the most incredible journeys, through dense jungle, up enormous mountains and across empty deserts. Keep treasures as you travel through the wilderness; memories of great conquests, brave rescues, laughter and fun. Decorate your favourite stick and let your memory mobile tell the tales.

HOW TO MAKE IT

1. Tie the end of the wool to one end of the stick. Hold the wool and twist the stick. The wool will wrap itself around the stick.

2. Make patterns by wrapping it closely or make stripes or criss-crosses by spreading it out. You can also thread beads on, or change the colour of your wool, by cutting it and tying a new piece on to the end of the last piece of wool.

3. Take each of your treasures and tie them to different-length pieces of wool. Attach them to your decorated stick as you like. You might want to hang your mobile up somewhere you can reach easily while you hang your treasures on it. This will help you to balance it out.

4. If you have a tricky-shaped treasure, you can wrap it up like a parcel with the garden wire and attach this to the piece of wool.

COLLECT TOGETHER

From nature:
A lovely stick about an arm's length long
Nature treasures from your journey

From the Out Pack:
Wool
Beads
Scissors
Garden wire

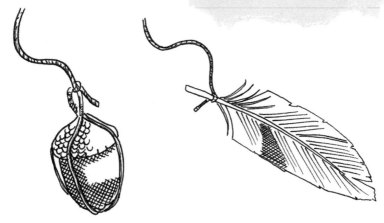

33

Mudasaurus

You'll know when you've found the very finest, squishiest, muddiest mud, so soft and brown and wet and muddy. There must be a gazillion different things you could make with this oozing squelch!

Imagine an enormous tail that swishes ...

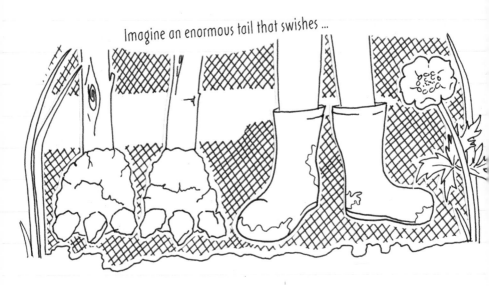

Can you imagine an enormous tail that swishes? With spines and claws and great pointy teeth? Yes, please make one of those for us. Your very own mudasaurus!

Here are some ideas for making different parts of a dinosaur. Put them together however you like ... Is yours a sticklodocus or treeceratops?

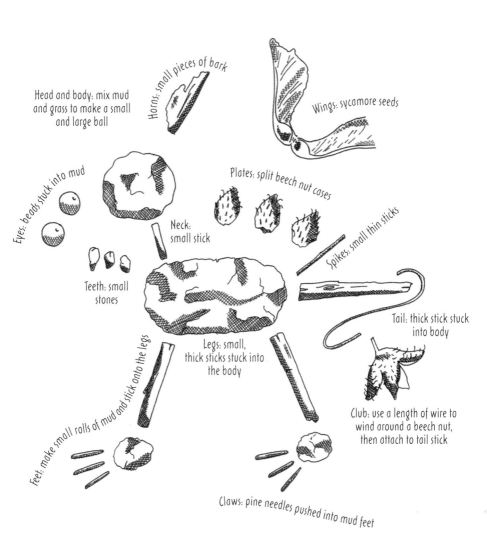

Horns: small pieces of bark

Head and body: mix mud and grass to make a small and large ball

Wings: sycamore seeds

Plates: split beech nut cases

Eyes: beads stuck into mud

Neck: small stick

Spikes: small thin sticks

Teeth: small stones

Tail: thick stick stuck into body

Legs: small, thick sticks stuck into the body

Feet: make small rolls of mud and stick onto the legs

Club: use a length of wire to wind around a beech nut, then attach to tail stick

Claws: pine needles pushed into mud feet

If you're in your backyard and the mud's looking a bit hard, why not give your mudasaurus a drink of water before you start? This will help him wake him up.

If you're in the forest and the mud is too wet, how about feeding your mudasaurus some grass to help him stand up?

Fairy Treehouse and Elf Garden

It is puzzling. Where do fairies live when they're not up chimneys taming monsters? Or when they're not lugging teeth back to the tooth mountain? And what about elves, who love to tend to the garden of an overworked fairy? There are surely lots of tree-trunk houses with stepladders and roof-top playgrounds and multi-coloured super-trampolines ... aren't there?

Window: Make a circle with a bendy stick and fix with tape. Lash two sticks across the circle. Thread leaves on to wire and bend and twist on to circle.

Ladder: Lash small sticks together, leaving a small gap between each.

Door: Lash small sticks together (see page 132). Thread a wire through a bead, then bend and twist on to door.

36

HOW TO MAKE THE SWING:

1. Lash two sticks together for each side and rest a longer stick on top.

2. Tie a hand-length of string to the top stick. Attach a leaf onto the string with masking tape.

COLLECT TOGETHER

From nature:
13 finger-length sticks
Longer stick
Leaf
Stone

From the Out Pack:
Wool
Masking tape
4 beads
Garden wire

HOW TO MAKE THE SLIDE:

1. Lash five sticks together and rest on a stone.

HOW TO MAKE THE ROUNDABOUT:

1. Lash four sticks together.

2. Thread four beads onto a hand-length of wire and bend and twist into a circle.

3. Push a finger-length stick through the middle of the sticks and into the circle of beads.

Wonky Racer

Take the lead, don't be
a chaser, make yourself
a wonky racer.

Wheels, axles and chassis' – or
should I say apples, twigs and
sticks? There's a brand new
racer somewhere outside, just
waiting for construction ...

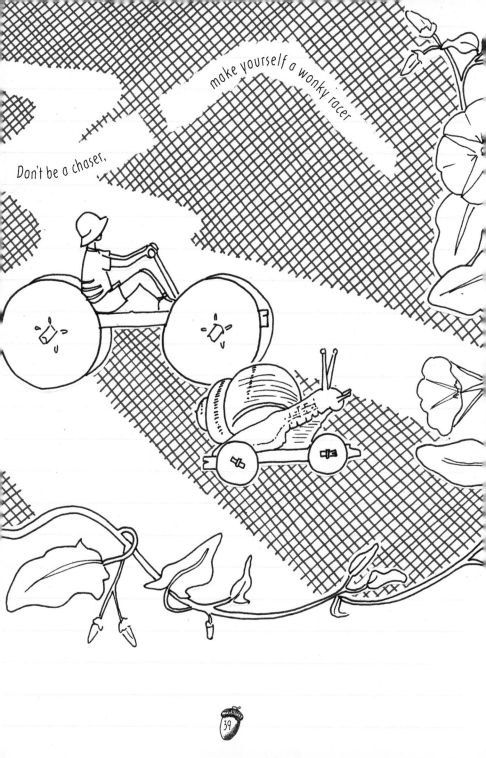

Wonky Racer No.1

COLLECT TOGETHER

From nature:

A finger-length stick

4 teeny tiny sticks, no bigger than your little finger nail

From the Out Pack:

4 big bumpy round beads

4 little round beads

Garden wire

HOW TO MAKE IT

1. Take an arm's length of garden wire, and halfway along, secure one of your teeny tiny sticks with a pinch and twist. Keep twisting the wire to make an axle, which is the length of a big and little bead together.

2. Thread your big bead and then your little bead onto the twisted wire.

3. Take your finger-length stick and secure it to your two beads with a pinch and twist.

4. With the remaining garden wire, pinch and twist and keep twisting to make the other side of the axle, which will be the length of another big and little bead. Thread on the beads.

5. Take another teeny tiny stick and secure this with a pinch and twist.

6. Repeat steps 1–5 at the other end of the stick and go racing.

Wonky Racer No.2

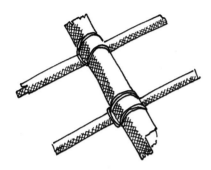

COLLECT TOGETHER

From nature:

A 2-hand length stick of about
   2 fingers thickness
2 finger sticks
4 fallen apples

From the Out Pack:

String
Elastic bands
Scissors

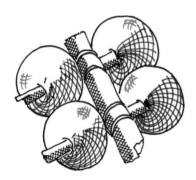

HOW TO MAKE IT

1. With two arm's lengths of string, lash (see skills section, page 132) your two smaller sticks tightly to each end of your big stick.

2. Push each of your four apples, right through the core, on to the four ends of your finger sticks.

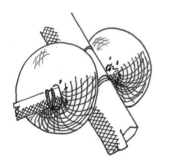

3. Twist an elastic band onto the finger sticks on either side of the car to stop the apples from falling off.

4. Go racing, but watch out for the juice factory!

Season Star

Summer, autumn, winter, spring ...
What's lying on the ground?
Decorate your season star
With whatever can be found ...

HOW TO MAKE IT

1. Take your five sticks and lash them at alternate ends so that they form a zig-zag. Use about an arm's length of string at each join.

2. Place them on the floor in a zig-zag so that the start of the zig-zag looks like a 'W'.

3. Take stick 1 and cross it over stick 3 to make your first star point.

4. Take stick 4 and cross it over sticks 1 and 2.

5. Take stick 5 behind the top point to complete your star. Lash sticks 1 and 5 together to make your final point.

COLLECT TOGETHER

From nature:
5 arm-length sticks
Anything nature has left on the ground

From the Out Pack:
String
Beads
Wool
Scissors

6. Take a three-arm's length of wool and wind it under and over the frame of your star. You can add strength to your star as you go by winding the wool around the sticks where they cross. You can also add beads for extra decoration.

7. Weave all the nature treasures that you've found in and out of your string to decorate your season star from top to bottom.

8. Hang your season star on your door so everyone can see the beauty of the season. Can you find a season star on anyone else's front door? Maybe they're an Outpacker too ...

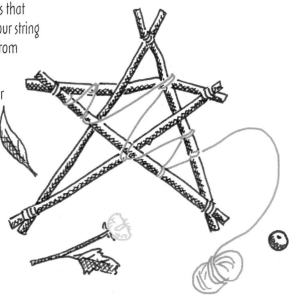

43

Blast Off

You'll love this nifty little way of making your own space rocket that you can launch. 5, 4, 3, 2, 1 ... Galacto Astro Fun!

5, 4, 3, 2, 1 ... Galacto Astro Fun!

COLLECT TOGETHER

From nature:

Hand-length stick of 3-finger thickness

2 finger-length pieces of elder wood
  (see page 121)

Leaves as red as you can find

1 big tough leaf

From the Out Pack:

A straightened paperclip

Masking tape

String

Pens

Scissors

2 beads

HOW TO MAKE IT

1. Take each piece of elder and carefully hollow out the centre of the stick by pushing your paperclip from one end to the other. Make this hole bigger by pushing a thin stick through the hole.

2. Take your hand-length stick and attach your fiery leaves to the base with masking tape.

3. Make your big tough leaf into a cone shape and attach this to the other end.

4. Place your two hollowed-out pieces of elder on the back of your rocket, about a finger-width apart. Attach them with two pieces of masking tape, each a finger-length long.

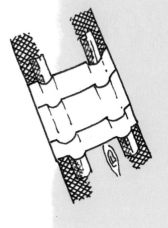

5. Take half an arm's length of masking tape and wrap it around both the rocket and your pieces of elder to make sure they're stuck on extra well.

6. Thread a three-arm's length of string up through one of your pieces of elder from the fire to the nose cone and back down through the other one; this will give you a loop and two tail ends.

7. Attach a bead to each end of your string.

8. Decorate your masking tape however you like.

9. Hook the loop of your string over a tree branch, a door handle, a fence – anything you can find. Pull the two beads apart and watch your rocket blast off.

Fire-breathing Dragon

Would you believe that beneath the heaps of
fallen autumn leaves, there's a fire-breathing
dragon who wants to be your friend?

He wants you to meet the knights
in acorn hats who look after him so
well. He wants to show you the secrets
of his far-away land. Be sure to search
well for him, high and low, around
every tree, under every leaf ... he's
yours and he's waiting, just for you.

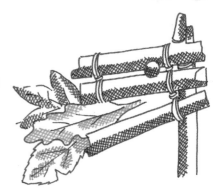

HOW TO MAKE IT

1. Lash the branched stick to
   one of the hand-length sticks.
   Then lash the remaining
   hand-length stick to these
   sticks, but only at one end.

2. Lash your arm-length stick to
   the back of your other sticks by
   the ear and the middle join.

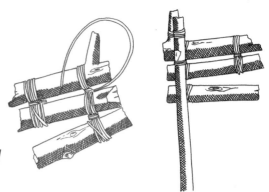

48

3. Take your bunch of fiery leaves and wrap the stems together with an arm's length of garden wire, leaving enough garden wire to attach your leaves to the bottom stick by wrapping it around.

4. Take a two-hand's length piece of garden wire and thread it through the small bead. Pinch and twist. Thread both ends of the wire through the big bead and attach it to one of the top sticks. This is your dragon's eye.

5. You can make your dragon open its mouth and breathe fire by tying a two-arm's length of string to the end of the bottom stick. Thread the string in between your sturdy stick and the ear of your top hand-length stick. Pull this and your dragon closes his mouth.

6. Make a harness for your dragon with plaited wool (see page 138) and go for a breath-taking ride through the clouds.

COLLECT TOGETHER

From nature:
A sturdy stick about an arm's length long
3 hand-length sticks, one with a side branch or 'ear'
A bunch of fiery leaves

From the Out Pack:
String
Garden wire
2 beads, one small, one big
Scissors
Wool

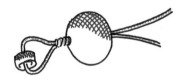

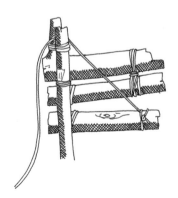

Rock Band

Set the stage, kill the lights and pull the curtain up.
Drum the beat of your nature jam, strum out some groovy
tunes, sing as high as the treetops and rock on ...

Guitar

COLLECT TOGETHER

From nature:
1 arm-length stick
2 sticks, wrist-to-elbow length
2 sticks, fingertip-to-elbow length

From the Out Pack:
String
Elastic bands

HOW TO MAKE IT

1. Take your arm-length stick and one of your wrist-to-elbow-length sticks. Lash (see skills section, page 132) the middle of the shorter stick near the bottom of the longer stick.

2. Take one of your fingertip-to-elbow-length sticks and lash the middle of this, a hand's length above the other.

3. Make a wonky square by lashing on your remaining sticks. This will make the shape of a proper electric guitar.

4. Take six elastic bands (or however many strings will fit on your guitar) to make the guitar strings and stretch them over your wonky square. Rock on.

Drum

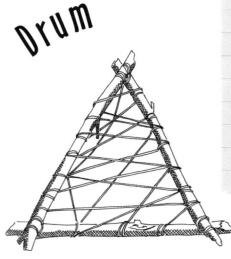

COLLECT TOGETHER

From nature:
3 sticks, wrist-to-elbow length
1 other stick for your drumstick
A handful of leaves stone

From the Out Pack:
String

What happens to the sound if you weave different leaves into the other side of your drum? Or tape together a few strands of grass and use these as your drumstick?

HOW TO MAKE IT

1. Lash your three sticks in a triangle shape.

2. Take a three-arm's length of string and tie the end onto one corner of your stick triangle. Criss-cross the string from one side to another until you reach the bottom corner.

3. Turn your triangle and criss-cross from bottom to top, making a tight mesh.

4. Weave your leaves through one side of your mesh.

5. Take your drumstick and rock on.

Rock Castanets

HOW TO MAKE IT

1. Take an arm's length of garden wire and place your large stone in the middle of it. Wrap the wire around the stone and secure with a pinch and a few twists.

2. Wrap the two ends of the wire back around the stone and feed each end of the wire underneath the first wire; secure with a pinch and twist. It should look like a ribbon wrapped around a present.

3. Do the same with the smaller stone.

COLLECT TOGETHER

From nature:
1 fist-sized stone
1 smaller, rounder stone

From the Out Pack:
Garden wire

4. Join the two stones by pinching and twisting all four wire ends.

5. Play by tapping them together. Viva España!

GRASS SQUEALER

HOW TO MAKE IT

1. Press the grass between the sides of your thumbs so that it is stretched tight.

2. Blow through the space left in the centre.

COLLECT TOGETHER

From nature:
1 shiny, thick blade of grass

3. Keep practising, as it really is a lot of fun once you get going. Squeal on!

Mud-pie Market

'Roll up, roll up, get your mud pies,
your mouth-watering mud pies. Get your welly
jelly beans, leaf toffee, pine-cone fizz balls,
sherbet acorns ... any delicious swizzilicious
sweet you can think of.'

'Give a shout, weigh them out and fizz, whizz,
the finest treats without a doubt.'

Mud-pie Market

HOW TO MAKE IT

1. Make an 'H'-shape by lashing two of
   the fingertip-to-elbow-length sticks and
   one of your hand-length sticks of finger
   thickness. Do this again so you've got
   two 'H's.

2. Take one 'H' and cross the top two
   ends to make an 'A'. Lash on another
   fingertip-to-elbow-length stick to make
   a teepee shape.

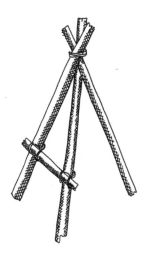

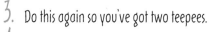

COLLECT TOGETHER

From nature:

6 fingertip-to-elbow-length sticks
   of 2-finger thickness
2 hand-length sticks of 1-finger thickness
2 arm-length sticks
Lots of hand-length sticks

From the Out Pack:

String
Scissors

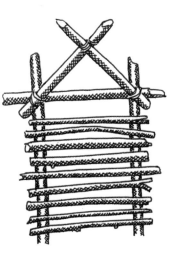

3. Do this again so you've got two teepees.

4. Take your two arm-length sticks and balance them between your two teepees.

5. Place all of your hand-length sticks along the two arm-length sticks to make your sweet-shop shelf.

Sweet-shop Scales

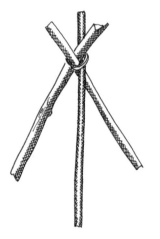

1. Take your fingertip-to-elbow-length sticks and a two-arm's length of string.

2. Lie your three sticks on the ground next to each other. Take your two-arm's length of string and tie a good knot around the end of the three sticks. Wrap the remaining string round and round the sticks and secure with another good, strong knot.

3. Spread the sticks out and place on the ground in a teepee shape.

4. Balance your arm-length stick on top of your tepee. It should rock like a scale.

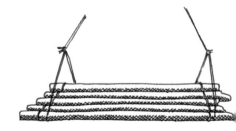

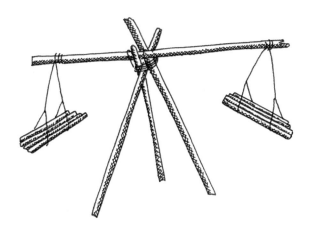

5. Make a scale pan by lashing five of your hand-length sticks together at each end. Repeat with the other five.

6. Take an arm's length of string and tie a knot around the scale pan at each end, leaving a loop in the middle for hanging off your scales. Repeat with the other scale pan.

7. Hang these from each end of your scales until they balance.

8. Loosely lash an arm's length of string where the scales rest on the teepee to stop them from falling off.

9. Collect whatever you can from nature that can be made into a delicious or yucky nature treat for your shop.

10. 'That'll be a 100g of leaf toffee please!'

Remember

Nature sweets sound yummy and mud-pie cakes look scrummy,

But please remember, don't eat them, they'll really hurt your tummy.

Puddle Pictures

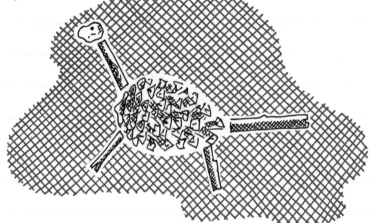

Take a peek into a puddle – there's
a whole other world down there.
The sort of world that you can
make any which way you like:
a leafy ballerina, a stickladocus,
bark boat or a jungle zoo. Take a
peek into a puddle. Which amazing
world is shining back at you?

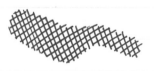

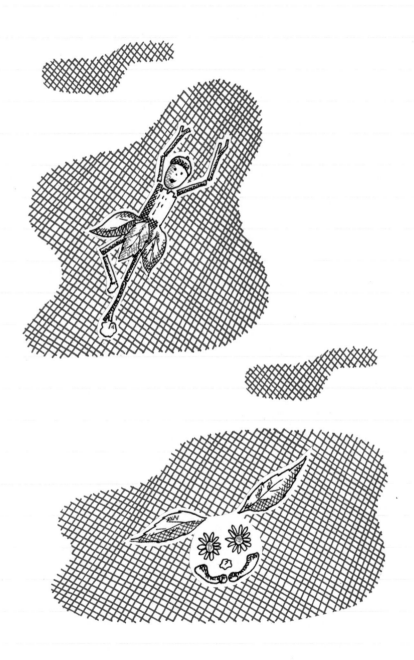

Magic

Acorn, root, sapling, tree ...
Out Pack magic 1, 2, 3 ...

We all know that nature is magic, probably the most magical thing in our whole enormous universe. But can you make nature into magic? Of course you can. Search for your wand, learn your nature tricks and wow everyone with your very own dazzling magic show.

The Magnetic Stick

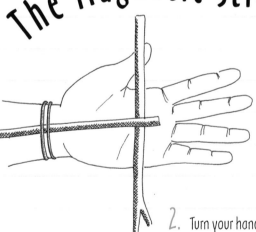

1. Away from your audience, place the two elastic bands or plaited bracelet around your wrist.

2. Turn your hand over, so your palm is facing upwards. Place your hand-length stick through the elastic bands so it comes almost to the top of your palm. This is your invisible stick.

3. Now it's time to start your show ...

4. Tell the audience that you are about to amaze them with your magnetic stick trick. Ask the audience to find a stick, nothing thicker than your finger.

5. Take the stick from them and place it in your hand. Without the audience noticing, slip the stick underneath your invisible stick. It will look as if you are just holding it.

6. Say the magic words.

   ' Acorn, root, sapling, tree ...
   Out Pack magic 1, 2, 3 ...'

7. Slowly open your hand to show the stick magically and magnetically staying in place without you holding it. Try to look as if you are using your mind to keep it in place.

8. Give your stick back to an audience member and while they look closely at the stick to check it, slip the invisible stick out from the elastic bands and drop it on the ground. Then you can turn your hand over to show them it's empty.

COLLECT TOGETHER

From nature:
1 hand-length stick, pencil thickness
Any stick as long as it's wider than your hand

From the Out Pack:
2 elastic bands or a plaited wool bracelet
   (see skills section, page 138)

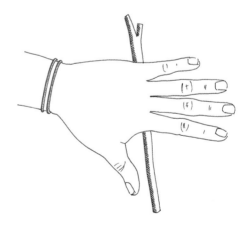

THE CLIMBING LEAF

HOW TO MAKE IT

1. Cut your elastic band.

2. Ask your audience to choose a leaf.

3. Using the garden wire, carefully poke a tiny hole through the centre of the leaf. Thread the elastic band through the leaf.

4. Secretly, keep at least half of the elastic band in your right hand.

5. Stretch the other half of the elastic, about a hand width, with your left hand. Make sure your left hand is higher than your right hand, giving the leaf a slope to climb.

6. Start the leaf next to your right hand.

7. Say the magic words:

   ' Acorn, root, sapling, tree ...
   Out Pack magic 1, 2, 3 ...'

8. Slowly let the elastic slide through the fingers of your right hand, keeping the distance between the two hands the same. The leaf should appear to be climbing up the elastic band.

9. Make sure you don't let go of either end of the elastic band.

THE MAGIC DISAPPEARING STICK

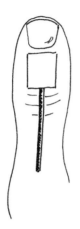

COLLECT TOGETHER

From nature:
1 tiny thin stick, about the length
of your thumb

From the Out Pack:
A very small square of masking tape

HOW TO MAKE IT

1. Away from the audience, stick the end of your tiny stick to the piece of masking tape.

2. Place this just above the knuckle of one of your thumbs, with the rest of the stick running down your thumb towards your hand, as shown above.

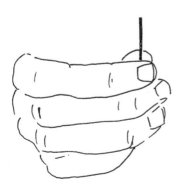

3. Bend your thumb until the stick is upright and put your fingers in front of your thumb to look as if you are just holding the stick. Make sure none of the masking tape is showing.

4. Now you are ready to show the audience your trick. Say the magic words:

   ' Acorn, root, sapling, tree ...
   Out Pack magic 1, 2, 3 ...'

5. Open your hand. This action will hide the stick behind your thumb. Your audience will be amazed – make a show of looking for and finding it, without showing the back of your hand.

The Out-Pack Games

'THERE'S FUN IN THE MAKING.'

Introduction to the Games

All the way around this great big world of ours, from the Inuit in their igloos to the Maohi in their beachside huts, there are people playing games. We humans just love them. And I'm pretty sure that you do too. What's especially lucky about this is that games are wonderfully good for us all. They help us to think, talk, move, laugh and so many other things that make us feel great.

Have a think about the games that you play. I bet you know lots: games that you can play inside and outside, and even on your head! But I wonder if you know any games that you can make out of nature. You might have heard of conkers or Poohsticks; these are fantastic games that you can make out of nature and this chapter gives you a whole lot more.

First, there are our games from the games kit. This is a collection of classics that are enjoyed the world over, as much in old times as new. The difference is that you

won't need to carry your rounders kit with you or bring your cricket bat. All you need to do is forage in nature, and with a few bits from your Out Pack to bind and stick, you'll have a games kit fit for a day of fun whether you're camping, at the park, at the beach or in your own backyard.

There are also some makey games, some sticky games and some thinky games. Plus there are some games that don't necessarily involve any winning or losing, so whatever your mood, whatever your day, there's plenty of fun to be had.

66

How to Pick Who Goes First

We've created a counting-out game for you to decide who takes the first turn in your games. Everyone who is going to play should put a hand into the middle of the group and one person should say the counting-out words, touching each person's hand on each word. The person whose hand is touched on 'ME' gets to take the first turn.

The counting-out words go like this:

Acorn, Root, Sapling, Tree,
Who is it?
It is ... ME!

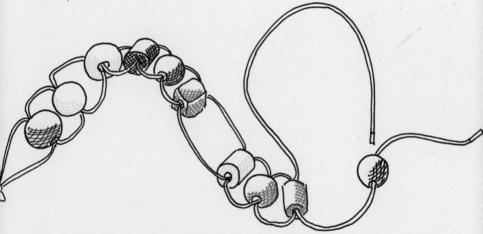

How to Keep Your Score

We know that it can be really hard to remember your score while you're playing a game, so here's how to make a counting string. Tie two pieces of string together at one end. Tape the loose ends with a small piece of masking tape. Take a bead and thread one piece of string through the hole. Thread the other piece of string through the bead but from the opposite direction. Repeat until you have 10 beads on your counting string. Tie a knot in the two loose ends, leaving some space to slide the beads along the string to keep your score.

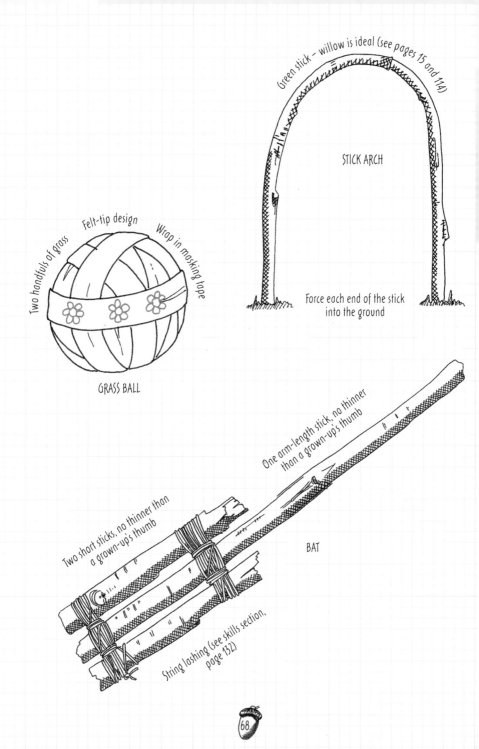

Green stick – willow is ideal (see pages 15 and 114)

STICK ARCH

Force each end of the stick
into the ground

Felt-tip design

Two handfuls of grass

Wrap in masking tape

GRASS BALL

One arm-length stick, no thinner
than a grown-up's thumb

BAT

Two short sticks, no thinner than
a grown-up's thumb

String lashing (see skills section,
page 132)

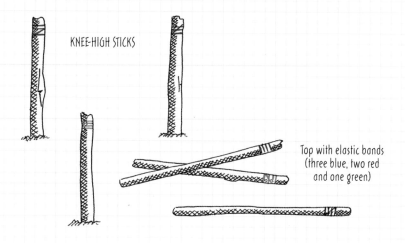

KNEE-HIGH STICKS

Top with elastic bands
(three blue, two red
and one green)

The Games Kit

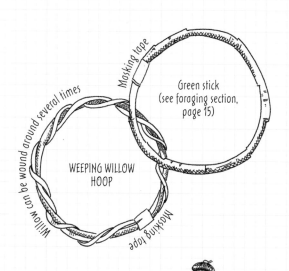

Masking tape

Green stick
(see foraging section,
page 15)

Willow can be wound around several times

WEEPING WILLOW
HOOP

Masking tape

Wobble Catch

How are you at catching a ball when you're on your knees and you've got a hand on your head? Catching and throwing and wibbling and wobbling: that's what this one's all about ...

Use the counting-out game to see who goes first (see page 67). Take turns throwing the ball to each other. The ball should be thrown towards the hands of the next player. If the ball is too high, low or wide, it's a 'no ball' and must be thrown again.

If the player catches the ball they then throw it on to the next player. If they don't catch it, there is a challenge:

Age range: Any age.

No. of people: At least 2.

Aim: To be the last person still in.

From the games kit: One grass ball.

Set-up: Players stand five steps apart, either facing each other or in a circle if there's more than two.

First dropped catch: The player must stand with their legs wide apart and stay like this for their next turn. If the player then catches the ball, they can stand normally again. If they don't catch it, there is another challenge:

Second dropped catch: The player must stand on one leg and stay like this for their next turn. If the player then catches the ball, they go back to standing with their legs wide apart. If they don't catch it, there is another challenge:

Third dropped catch: The player must drop down to their knees and stay like this for their next turn. If the player then catches the ball, they go back to standing on one leg. If they don't catch it, there is a final challenge:

Winner: The winner is the last one out, even if they're on their knees with their hand on their head!

More or less of a challenge?

Fourth dropped catch: The player must now place one hand on their head and stay like this for their next turn. If the player then catches the ball, they go back to catching the ball on their knees but with both hands. If they don't catch it, they're out!

Players can stand further apart or you can include closing your eyes. Or make it a bit easier by having an adult throw the ball.

Nature Boules

A great and powerful genie has escaped from his lamp. Bigger than the moon and stars, he picks up two planets and throws them as close as he can to the sun. That's because he's playing a game called Galacto Astro Boules – a similar game to the one simply called boules, loved as much by the French as by great and powerful genies. You can enjoy this game too, but instead of planets you can use your grass balls and bits and pieces from nature.

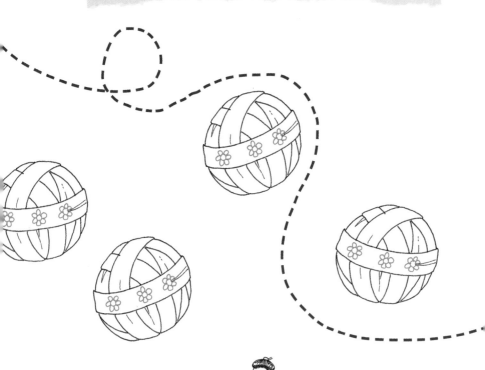

Set-up: Place your 'starting stick' on the ground. Find a 'nature jack' such as a conker or a pine cone – anything that is not going to blow away. Stand behind your starting stick and throw the nature jack a short distance.

Start: Use the counting-out game to see who goes first (see page 67). Standing behind the starting stick, each player takes a turn at throwing one of their boules as close as they can to the nature jack. Once all the players have taken their two turns, check whose boule is closest to the nature jack.

Winner: The winner is the player who managed to get their boule closest to the nature jack.

Age range: Any age.

No. of people: Any number.

Aim: To throw your 'boules' as close to the 'nature jack' as possible.

From the games kit: Two grass balls per player, individually decorated. These are your boules.

More or less of a challenge?

Start again or keep the score over a number of rounds. Swap it round by making your grass ball the 'jack' and using different items from nature as your boules. Is a feather harder to throw than a beech nut?

French Cricket

In the game of cricket, it is the batter's job to protect his wicket. A bit like when a knight defends his princess or a pirate guards his treasure. In French Cricket it's all about your legs, so protect them well ...

Age range: Any age.

No. of people: At least 2.

Aim: To not get 'out'.

From the games kit: The bat and a grass ball.

Set-up: The batter stands with their feet together and their bat in front of their legs. The bowler stands five paces in front of the batter. The other players take positions around the batter at least five paces away. They are the fielders.

Start: Use the counting-out game to see who bats first (see page 67). The bowler throws the ball, underarm, towards the batter's legs and below the knees. The batter tries to hit the ball as far as they can away from the bowler or fielders.

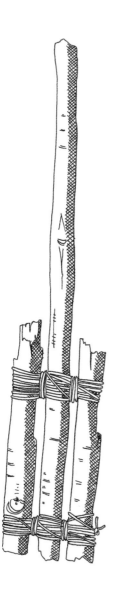

- The batter must not move their feet throughout their turn.

- The bowler must bowl the ball from wherever it lands, even if this is behind the batter. If this happens, the batter must twist around to try to hit the ball without moving their feet.

The batter is 'out' if:

- The bowler or a fielder catches the ball before it hits the ground.

- The ball hits them on the legs below the knees. They are not out if the ball has hit the bat before it hits their legs.

The next batter is the player who got the previous player 'out'.

Winner: The batter who stays in for the longest time.

A Bit Like Croquet

This is a lot like, but not altogether like,
which is why it's only a bit like croquet.

Aim: To be the first person to hit your
ball through the arches in the right
order and then hit the finishing stick.

From the games kit: A grass ball for
each player, individually decorated;
five arches, numbered 1-5; one
knee-high stick to be the finishing
stick and the bat.

Set-up: Position a leaf, the arches and
finishing stick in an 'S'-shape, as
illustrated.

Start: Use the counting-out game to see
who goes first. Each player, in turn, places
their ball on the starting leaf and hits
the ball through the first hoop. If it goes
through, they get another hit towards the
second hoop. If they miss, the turn goes
to the next player, who starts from the
starting leaf.

If the balls hit each other, don't worry,
just hit them from their new positions.

Once a player has hit their ball through
all of the arches they must hit the
finishing stick to complete the round.

Winner: The first player to hit the
finishing stick.

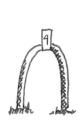

FINISH

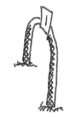

STICK ARCHES
(see games kit,
page 68)

masking tape numbers

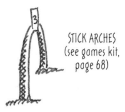

START

More or less of a challenge?

Younger children could have an extra hit per turn. To make it more challenging, try to hit the ball through the arches in both directions, make the course longer or put in obstacles.

Rounders

Run, run as fast as you can ...
All the way round and don't get stumped,
That way they won't catch you, gingerbread man!

A rounder is when a batter runs around all of the
bases in one go without being stumped – a simple
whack-the-ball-and-run game that can keep heaps
of you entertained for hours.

Age range: Any age.

No. of people: At least 8.

Aim: To be the team with the most 'rounders'.

From the games kit: Four hoops, four arches, the bat and a grass ball.

Set-up: Set out the four bases, bowling stick and batting stick as illustrated. Divide your group into two teams. The team with the youngest player decides who bats first.

One player from the batting team stands behind the batting stick with the bat. This is the batter. The rest of the batting team stands a safe distance away from the batter and the bases.

The fielding team picks positions; one bowler, one backstop (this is the player who stands behind the batter), four fielders to stand at the bases and as many fielders spread out in the field as you have. The bowler stands behind the bowling stick.

Start: The bowler throws the ball, underarm, towards the batter. Any throw that is too high, low, wide or close is a 'no ball' and must be bowled again.

The batter tries to hit the ball as far as they can. If they miss the ball they can have a further two turns before they must run to the first base. They must drop the bat before they run.

When the next batter hits the ball and runs to the first base, the player who went before them must run to the second base or further on if it's safe.

How a batter is out:

• One of the fielders catches the ball before it hits the ground.

• If a batter leaves their base and runs towards the next, they may be stumped out by anyone on the fielding team touching the base with the ball. They may also return to the base that they've run from if there's no one else on it.

Once the batter passes fourth base they can re-join their team and have another go when it's their turn.

The batting team continues batting until everyone in the team is out. The teams then swap.

Winner: The winning team is the one with the most rounders.

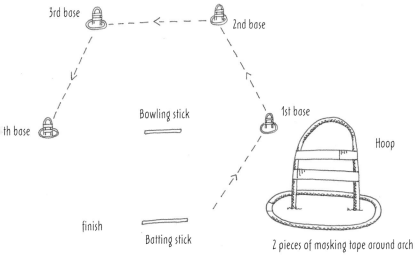

3rd base

2nd base

Bowling stick

1st base

Hoop

th base

finish

Batting stick

2 pieces of masking tape around arch

79

Hoopla

Get the hoop over the stick ... that's it!.

Age range: Any age.

No. of people: Any number.

Aim: To score the most points by throwing the hoops over the knee-high sticks.

From the games kit: 5 hoops and 6 coloured knee-high sticks.

Set-up: Place the knee-high sticks in a triangle format, and the starting stick five paces away, as illustrated.

Start: Use the counting-out game to see who goes first (see page 67). The first player stands behind the starting stick and tries to throw the five hoops over the sticks. Each player takes a turn.

Scoring:

The green stick is 1 point.
The red sticks are 2 points each.
The blue sticks are 3 points each.

Winner: The player with the most points when everyone's taken a turn.

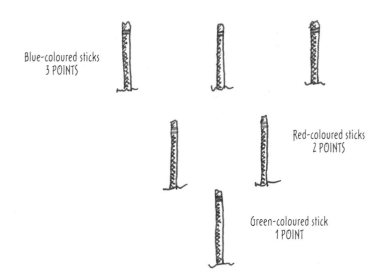

Blue-coloured sticks
3 POINTS

Red-coloured sticks
2 POINTS

Green-coloured stick
1 POINT

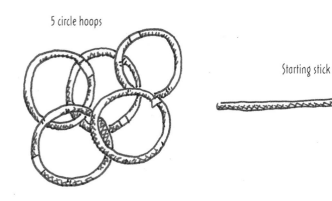

5 circle hoops

Starting stick

More or less of a challenge?

You can either start again or keep count over a number of rounds.
What happens if you make the hoops smaller? What happens if you
make the sticks smaller? Or if you stand further away? Or if you use
your left hand – or your right one?

Obstacle Course

Gather together all the parts of your games kit and arrange it as you can see in the picture or in your own cleverer way. Ask a grown-up to time you as you zoom round the obstacles. In and out and up and down, crab walk, hop and stop, lovely day, wobble egg ... hooray!

Age range: Any age.

No. of people: Any number.

Aim: To get round quicker than you did last time.

From the games kit: Everything.

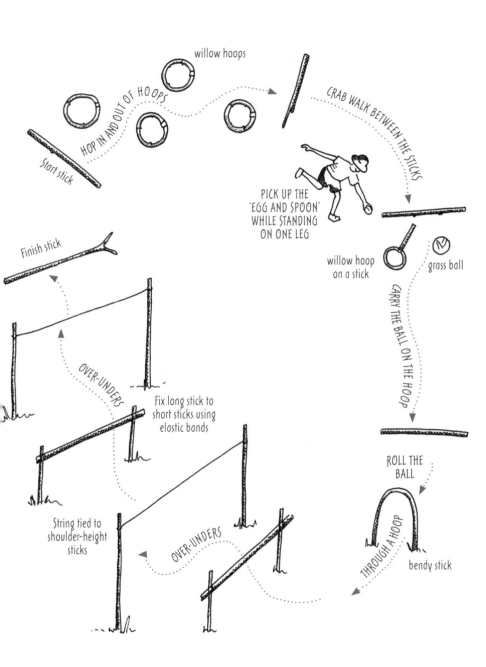

willow hoops

HOP IN AND OUT OF HOOPS

Start stick

CRAB WALK BETWEEN THE STICKS

PICK UP THE 'EGG AND SPOON' WHILE STANDING ON ONE LEG

willow hoop on a stick

grass ball

CARRY THE BALL ON THE HOOP

Finish stick

OVER-UNDERS

Fix long stick to short sticks using elastic bands

ROLL THE BALL

String tied to shoulder-height sticks

OVER-UNDERS

THROUGH A HOOP

bendy stick

Makey Games and Sticky Games

At the bottom of the deep blue ocean,

next to a twinkling coral reef

Neptune's Fishing Game

At the bottom of the deep blue ocean, next to a twinkling coral reef, there's a bright sunlit sand patch where Neptune, God of the Sea is playing his favourite game ...

Age range: Any age.

No. of people: Probably no more than 8 children.

Neptune has collected some nature treasures from a nearby wood and is making as many sea creatures as he can. So far he's got:

1 sparkling leaf fish
1 willow jellyfish
1 starfish of twigs and
1 horse-chestnut shark

Neptune's very favourite bit is when he tries to catch the creatures using his stick and pine-cone fishing rod. Quick, see if you can out-do Neptune and add some more sea creatures to the list – he hasn't thought of a wild-flower mermaid or a bark whale just yet. Oh, and don't forget to go fishing ... it's very catchy.

Make sure you look at Neptune's Rules on page 89.

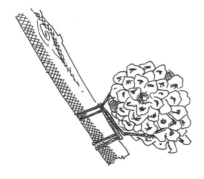

COLLECT TOGETHER

From nature:
Stick
Pine cone
Leaves
Grasses
Wild flowers

From the Out Pack:
String
Garden wire
Paperclips
Bead
Scissors

HOW TO MAKE THE ROD

1. Cut half an arm's length of garden wire and secure it around one of the pine cones with a pinch and twist.

2. Lash (see skills section, page 132) the pine cone to one end of your stick so that it's securely attached. Do this on the other end.

3. Cut a two-arms' length of string. Tie the paper clip to one end of the string.

4. Make the paperclip into a hook by pulling out the long end. Thread a big bead on to the string as a weight for your fish hook.

5. Thread the string through the pine cones and along the stick to make your fishing rod.

Let's have a sneaky peek at Neptune's ideas so far ...

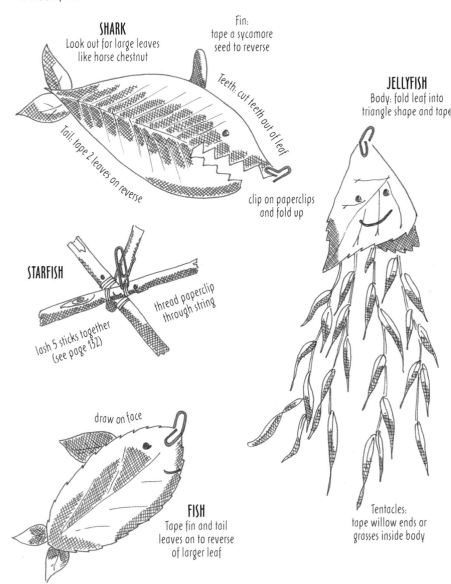

SHARK
Look out for large leaves like horse chestnut

Fin:
tape a sycamore seed to reverse

Teeth: cut teeth out of leaf

Tail: tape 2 leaves on reverse

clip on paperclips and fold up

JELLYFISH
Body: fold leaf into triangle shape and tape

STARFISH

lash 5 sticks together (see page 132)

thread paperclip through string

draw on face

FISH
Tape fin and tail leaves on to reverse of larger leaf

Tentacles:
tape willow ends or grasses inside body

Neptune's Rules

Start: Use the counting out game to see who goes first (see page 67). Each player takes a turn to catch as many sea creatures as they can in one minute. Both hands should be on the fishing rod while fishing. After each turn, throw the sea creatures back into the sea. Keep your score on your counting string.

Winner: The winner is the player who catches the most sea creatures. Take as many turns as you like. Remember, practice makes perfect.

Aim: To catch as many of Neptune's sea creatures as you can in the set time.

Set-up: Arrange Neptune's sea creatures on the ground with their paperclip hooks pointing up.

More or less of a challenge?

Fish can be different point values depending on how difficult they are to catch. For example the starfish could be one point as its paperclip is on the top of the fish. You can alter the position of the paperclips to make them harder to catch.

Sticky-bud Tails

Just imagine that you and all your friends have grown beautiful, long, green tails. Tails fit for any dragon, monster or dinosaur. Which do you think you might be today? You choose. Now imagine that each of your tails is a magic tail, and with every tail you collect, the faster you can run.

What are Sticky Buds?

This game uses a plant called goose grass that grows in late spring and summer. It is found in hedgerows and fields and it sticks to your clothes with harmless little hooks that are found on its leaves. It's a bit like Velcro.

Long sticky stems

Seeds with hooked hairs

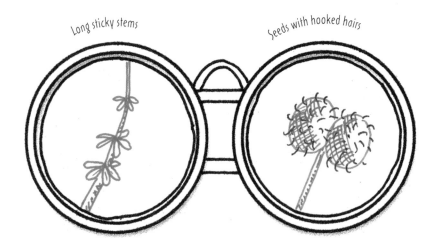

Set-up: Each player has an arm's length tail of goose grass, stuck to the back of their trousers or top. If the goose grass doesn't stick well on to your clothing, you can make a plaited tail (see skills section, page 138) that can be tucked into a waistband or belt of string.

Start: Each player should find a space away from the other players. On 'GO' they should start running, trying to catch the other players' tails without letting anyone catch theirs. They cannot hide or hold on to their own tails. If a player's tail is caught, they must sit down.

Winner: The last one standing wins!

Age range: Any age.

No. of people: Any number.

Aim: Run and try to collect everyone's tail – see how fast your legs will take you. But be careful that no one gets your tail, for your magic power will be gone and you'll need a little sit down. At the end of the game, aim to be the player who still has a tail.

More of a challenge?

Try playing 'sticky-bud tag', where one piece of sticky bud is used to show that someone is 'it' and gets passed from player to player, as in the traditional game of 'tag'.

91

Games For One

Oh no, you want to play a game and there's
no one with any spare time to play with you.
Don't worry, try one of these.

Sticky spider catch

I wonder if you've ever noticed that
house spiders don't look like houses
and money spiders don't look like
money. Well don't worry, because
pine-cone spiders are just as you'd
imagine, and they're especially fond
of leafy flies. When your pine-cone
spider has come to life, see if you can
help him get back to his web to eat his
luscious leafy fly dinner.

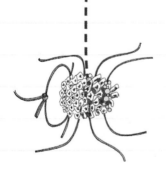

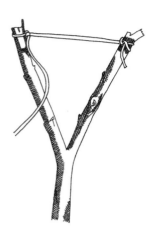

From nature:	From the Out Pack:
Y-shaped stick	String
Smallish pine cone	Garden wire
Small leaves	Elastic bands
	Beads
	Paperclips
	Masking tape
	Scissors

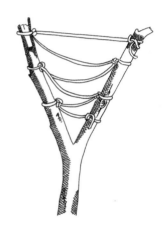

HOW TO MAKE THE WEB

1. Cut a two-arm's length piece of string. Tie a fish-on-a-dish knot (see skills section, page 130) on to the top of one arm of your 'Y'-shaped stick.

2. Pull the string over to the top of the other arm of the 'Y' and tie it securely.

3. Zigzag the string from one arm to the other. This bit needs to be a bit like a basket, so keep the string loose. Keep double knotting on each side and make sure the knots are nice and tight. Stop when you reach the bottom of the 'Y'.

4. Cut a further two-arm's length of string.

5. Tie this piece of string to the zigzag with single knots around the zigzag until it looks a bit like a spider's web.

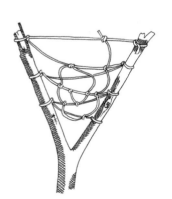

93

HOW TO MAKE THE SPIDER

1. Now carefully cut four pieces of garden wire, each about the length of two hands.

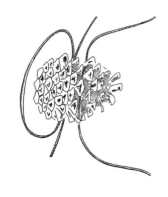

2. Wrap two of the wires around the pine cone and pinch and twist for legs. Make your spider's feet by folding the end of the wire back on itself and secure with a pinch and twist.

3. To make the eyes, thread eight beads (yes, most spiders have eight eyes!) into the middle of the next piece of wire, and wrap around the top of the pine cone with a pinch and twist. The ends are legs.

4. Cut five elastic bands and tie them together to make a bungee cord for the spider.

5. Tie one end of the bungee cord onto the last piece of garden wire and attach with a pinch and twist to the middle of the pine cone.

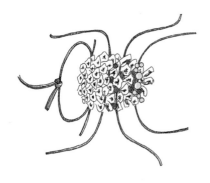

6. Tie the other end of the bungee securely to the top of one of the arms of your 'Y'-shaped stick.

7. You can make each fly for your spider to eat by picking two small leaves, placing them into a paperclip and adding a masking-tape face.

8. Now give your spider a helping hand with catching his leafy flies.

94

Hit it, bounce it

Think of a yo-yo, but instead of a yo-yo, you have a grass ball and elastic bands. You can hit it and bounce it and bounce it and hit it ... all day long.

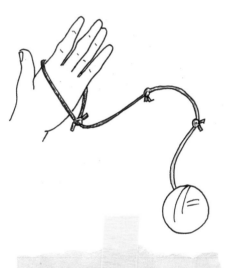

HOW TO MAKE IT

1. Take one grass ball and three of the elastic bands.

2. Cut the elastic bands and tie them to each other with knots to make a bungee cord.

3. Take two more elastic bands and tie them to the ends of your bungee cord.

4. Wrap one of the elastic bands tightly around the ball and place the other around your hand. Then hit the ball and bounce it. Fun!

COLLECT TOGETHER

From nature:
1 grass ball

From the Out Pack:
5 elastic bands

Skip 'n' hop

Skipperty, jumperty, hipperty, hopperty ... how many
times can you skip, jump, hip and hop your grass ball?

COLLECT TOGETHER

From nature:
1 small willow shoot
1 grass ball

From the Out Pack:
String
Scissors

DON'T TRIP OR STOP, JUST SKIP 'N' HOP!

1. Make a small woven hoop with a shoot of willow (see page 69). It should be big enough to pull over your foot but small enough that it won't fall off your ankle.

2. Attach an arm's length of string to the hoop, and on the other end attach a grass ball (see page 68).

3. Place the hoop over your foot.

4. Try to jump over the string as the ball circles around your foot. You'll need to make a big energetic circle with your foot to get the ball going.

5. There will be a good deal of jumping, hopping, skipping and laughing. Round and round and round ...

Out and Abouts

Wherever you are – your garden, the park, or in the middle of a beautiful forest – take a look around and see what you can find. Just imagine that every single tiny bit of nature that you can see – every plant, tree, animal, bug or fungus – has its own name, its own special features and a whole set of things that it likes and doesn't like. Every tiny part of nature is a lot like you!

Out and Abouts are here to introduce you to some of this beautiful nature. They're here to help you to look, see, make friends with and remember forever many of the fantastic things you will find outdoors. They do this by using some silly rhymes, funny jokes and lots of pretty pictures.

So when you're out and about, the best thing to do first of all is to check out which season it is. Do you remember your season rhyme? (see page 18). Trees and plants can look very different depending on the season. Many of them are dressed up for the party in summer, with their leaves, nuts, catkins and seeds, yet in winter time they are completely bare. Their crooked arms outstretched, probably reaching for a blanket to warm themselves up!

Once you've found your season, take a look at the flora and fauna in that section and then go on an adventure. We've chosen the most common ones for this country so you shouldn't have to go too far to find and make friends with them. Go on, go out and poke an oak. You never know, he might tell you a joke ...

Autumn

Trees

Our three autumn trees are deciduous –
they will lose all their leaves by
winter-time. They all have special nuts and
seeds so finding them should be no tricky
task for an Outpacker...

A nut with a hat

Cloud-shaped leaves

Oak Tree

Poke the oak and he
might tell you a joke...

Knock knock
Who's there?
Acorn
Acorn who?
Acorn remember!

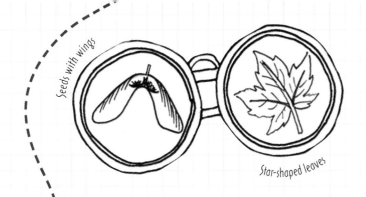

Seeds with wings

Star-shaped leaves

Sycamore

(Pick up a winged seed)
The sycamore is sick no more;
Here is the air ambulance
(throw your seed in the air).

The sad horse chestnut,
Waves his leaf fingers,
For his lost conkers.

Horse Chestnut

Leaves like hands

Shiny brown conkers in a spikey case

Fungi

It's hard to believe but fungi are more like us humans than plants and flowers. With a little to eat, drink and breathe they can get growing. You'll mainly find them on the sides of trees or coming out of the ground. They can be wibbly and wobbly, puffy and a bit curious. Have a good look but remember... Fungi, fungi never touch. They can hurt you very much.

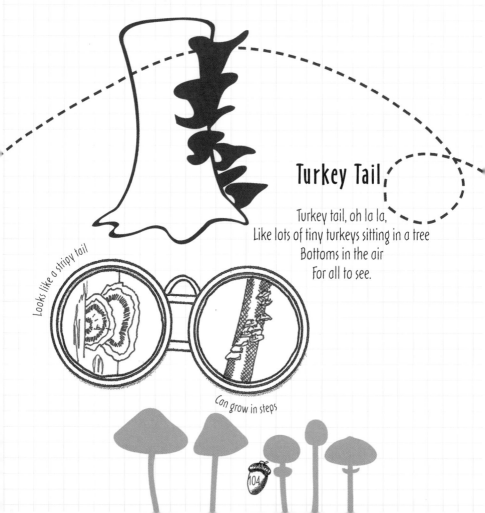

Turkey Tail

Turkey tail, oh la la,
Like lots of tiny turkeys sitting in a tree
Bottoms in the air
For all to see.

Looks like a stripy tail

Can grow in steps

Shaped like an ear

Grow on wood

Jelly Ear

What do you call a fungus that wobbles
like a jelly and is shaped like an ear?
Anything you like, it can't really hear you!

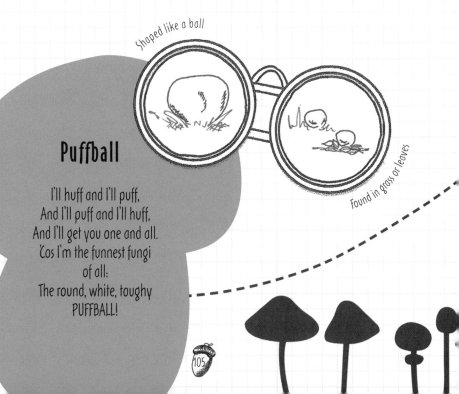

Shaped like a ball

Found in grass or leaves

Puffball

I'll huff and I'll puff,
And I'll puff and I'll huff,
And I'll get you one and all.
'Cos I'm the funnest fungi
of all:
The round, white, toughy
PUFFBALL!

Birds of a feather

Next time you see a black bird have a closer look. Was it crow, was it a jackdaw or was it a sneaky rook?

Crow

Glossy black carrion crow

Crea, crea, crea

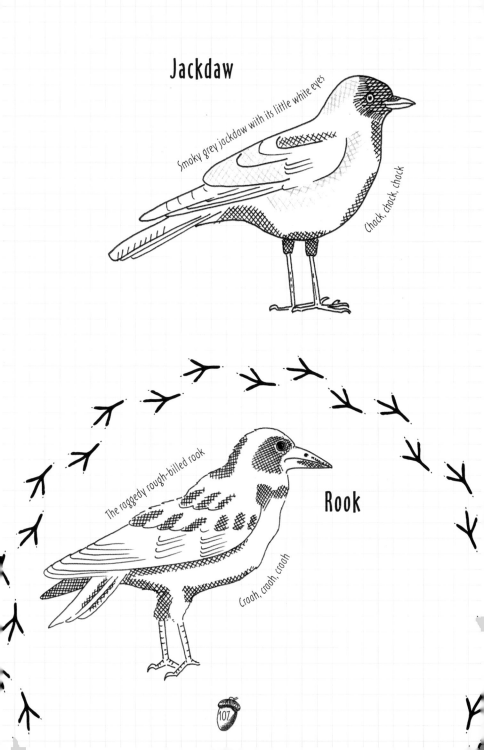

Jackdaw

Smoky grey jackdaw with its little white eyes

Chack, chack, chack

The raggedy rough-billed rook

Rook

Craah, craah, craah

Winter

Trees

Winter trees are trickier to spot unless they still have lots of their needles and pine cones on, like the Scots pine. For the others you'll have to have a really good look at their bark and perhaps a little look at the ground underneath them to see if they have left you any clues.

Silver Birch

Drooping silver birch shines bright with its peeling bark of white

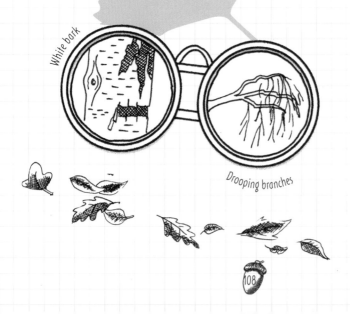

White bark

Drooping branches

Beech

What is grey and wrinkly and
stands in the woods?
No it's not your dad!
It has a trunk, but makes no sound.
No, it's not an elephant
playing hide and seek –
it's a beech tree!

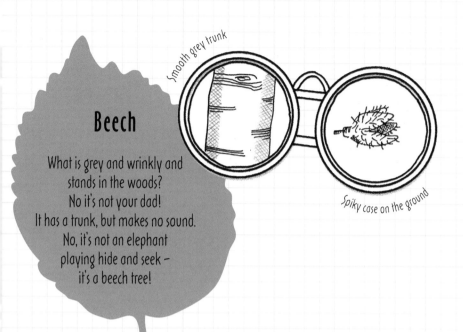

Smooth grey trunk

Spiky case on the ground

Scots Pine

My hair is thick with needles that I try to keep all year.
I've also got some cones that if you catch I'll give a cheer.
At Christmas time the other trees are sleeping, cold and bare,
But I'm all dressed for Santa with my needles in my hair.

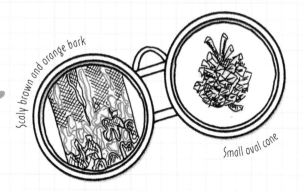

Scaly brown and orange bark

Small oval cone

Animals

Animals can often be quite shy of us out in nature so you may have to look for other signs that they've been out and about. Can you can find any tracks in the mud and figure out whose are whose? Or can you find something that they might have eaten?

Follow the animal tracks to find what they have left behind.

Rabbit

Squirrel

Mouse

Who's a messy eater?
Look at this roughly
eaten pine cone.

These are tidy eaters
– just a little munch.

This animal doesn't
leave much behind –
a hungry little racer.

Bugs

Bugs are tough, which is why there are such a lot of them. Under stones and logs and leaves and rocks, you won't have to go far to find these three busy at work. But be sure to put the roof back on their home when you say goodbye.

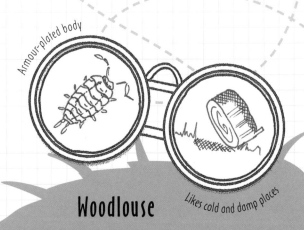

Armour-plated body

Likes cold and damp places

Woodlouse

Who's like a knight with his armour so tight,
And doesn't like places where light is so bright?
He lives in the woods,
And he lives in your house ...
It's the slow but strong woodlouse!

Centipedes

Like dinosaurs long past,
the centipede, a carnivore,
moves along so very fast.

Body in bits

Similar head and tail

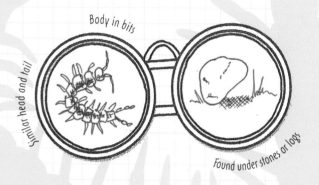

Found under stones or logs

Legs like hairs

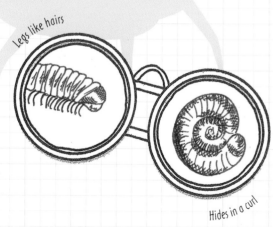

Millipedes

The millipede, a veggie,
with legs you cannot see,
moves along more slowly –
he doesn't chase his tea.

Hides in a curl

Spring

Trees

In spring, all the little buds are unfolding all over our bare trees. Catkins, blossom and tiny new shoots will show you the way to finding these three beauties.

Weeping Willow

Never fear, the weeping willow sheds no tears.
Like a fountain stretching over time,
Shoots so green, so long and fine.
By the water's edge her joy does call.
Remember, the willow doesn't weep at all.

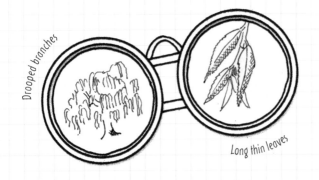

Drooped branches

Long thin leaves

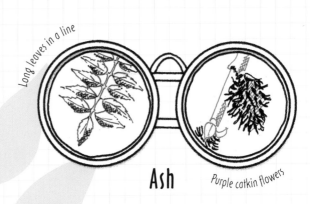

Long leaves in a line

Ash

Purple catkin flowers

Knock, knock.
Who's there?
Ash.
Ash who?
Bless you, it must be my catkins!

Spiky little tree

Crab Apple

Pink or white flowers

A thousand pretty flowers grow upon this little tree,
And each one makes an apple that you can't eat for your tea.
But boil them with some sugar and get ready for the WHAM!
For who'd have thought a crab apple could leave us in a jam.

Flowers

When you find a field of wild spring
flowers it's like finding a perfect rainbow.
Crisp and bright, a pure delight...

Remember,

These lovely flowers are very bright, but they'll give your tummy
quite a fright ... remember don't ever take a bite

Snowdrop

Head drop
Glow drop
Bell drop
Snowdrop

Nodding white flower

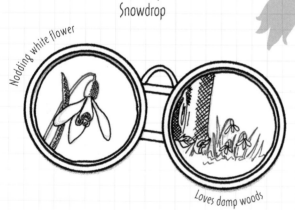

Loves damp woods

116

What small blue meadow
flower dreams of entering
the Olympics?
The Speedwell!

Speedwell

Sky-blue flowers

Loves grassy places

Bell-shaped flowers

Likes woodlands

Bluebell

Have you ever seen a carpet
running round the trees?
A woodland ocean, twinkling blue,
right up to your knees?
It's the story of a perfect flower,
so many people tell.
A tale of spring, a ding-a-ling,
the mild, the sweet bluebell.

Butterflies

Dashes of colour and brightness fluttering about... softy, gently, sweetly. When they're out they're easy to spot but can you tell one from another?

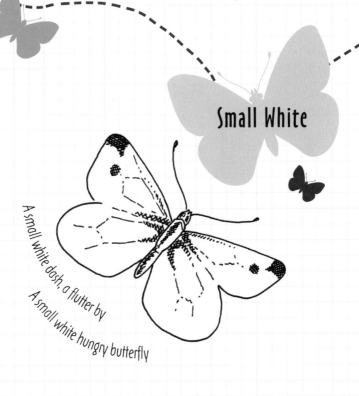

Small White

A small white dash, a flutter by
A small white hungry butterfly

Red Admiral

The stripy one with a body of dark night

Painted Lady

Spotty like a speckled beam of light

Summer

Trees

Summer trees are thick with life. They're bushy, green and lush. You shouldn't have any trouble finding these three.

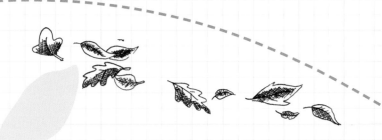

Rowan

Rowan, rowan where are you going?
You look a bit small and green.
Put on your bunches of bright red berries,
It's time for tea with the Queen!

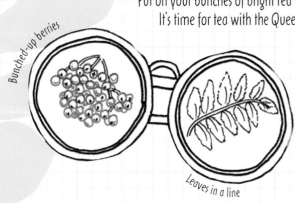

Bunched-up berries

Leaves in a line

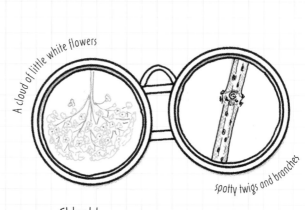

A cloud of little white flowers

spotty twigs and branches

Elder

This is an excited Elder tongue twister – say it as many times as you can. If you find it too easy, try to say it as fast as you can.

Elder blossom white, elder berry black

Again, again, again!

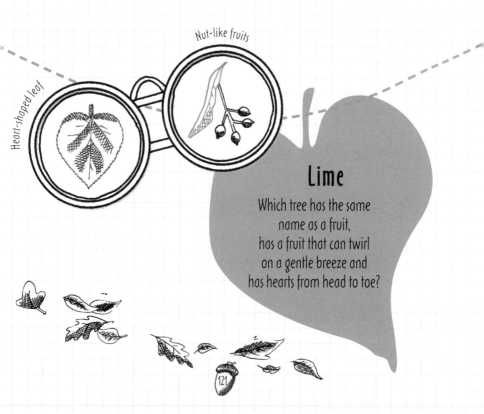

Nut-like fruits

Heart-shaped leaf

Lime

Which tree has the same name as a fruit, has a fruit that can twirl on a gentle breeze and has hearts from head to toe?

Flowers

Summer flowers are the bright flashes of colour in the thick fields of summer grass. These quirky three can be found easily in parks, meadows and back yards.

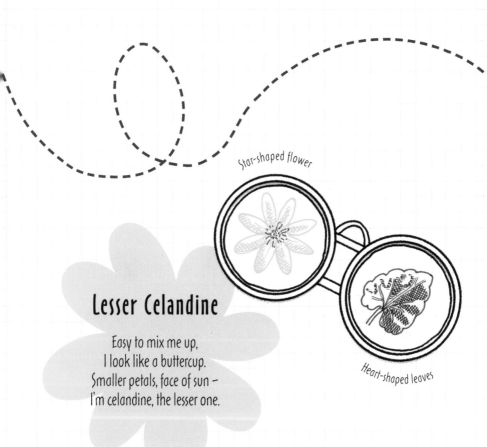

Star-shaped flower

Heart-shaped leaves

Lesser Celandine

Easy to mix me up,
I look like a buttercup.
Smaller petals, face of sun –
I'm celandine, the lesser one.

Cup-shaped flower

Likes the grass

Buttercup

Under the chin, see it glow,
If you like butter, we will know!

Clover

There once was a flower called clover,
Who wanted a total makeover.
He gelled up his hair to give it some flair ...
Now the bees rub their tummies all over.

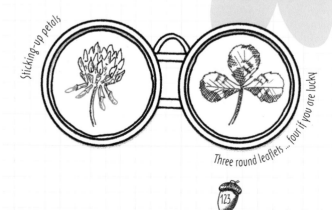

Sticking-up petals

Three round leaflets ... four if you are lucky!

Clouds

Cumulonimbus

Towering cumulonimbus cloud,
makes the thunder really loud

The sky is full of magic.
It's a really big clue to our
weather and changes all day
every day. It can create some of
the most beautiful colours, shapes
and patterns on our earth. So don't
forget to look up and take it in from
time to time. And just see if you can figure
out what the clouds are up to today...

Cirrus

Wispy one, high up to catch the sun

Cumulus

White and fluffy candyfloss

Nimbostratus

The grey, rainy blanket

Skills

Skills are fantastic things to have.
If you look after them well, they will stay with you
for the rest of your life.

They are not things you can keep in a box or in your Out Pack though. They are not heavy or soft or fragrant or loud. Skills are the wonderful things that you can learn to do with different parts of your body; sometimes just with your fingers and at other times with your arms, legs, teeth and eyebrows all at the same time! The skills in this section will make your creations and games kit stronger and easier to make, they will help you to climb trees and teach you how to survive out in nature.

Have a look at how you make a classic raft. Maybe you've made one already. In the instructions it says to tie a fish-on-a-dish knot. Well when you learn how to tie a fish-on-a-dish knot, it means that you've learned a skill. And this is a skill that might help you tie up your own boat one day.

Skills are such useful things to have and I'm sure you'll really enjoy learning them. But remember that they can sometimes be tricky to master, so don't worry if it's hard the first time that you do them. They need plenty of practice and you will probably discover that even your parents find them hard to do straight away.

Keep trying; you will think they are brilliant once you get the hang of them!

Fish-on-a-Dish Knot

This is a fantastic knot that is useful for all sorts of things. It is just as it sounds: you put your fish on your dish and you've got it. And just in case you hear someone saying something about a clove hitch, don't worry, that's what grown-ups call a fish-on-a-dish knot. Not nearly as good!

HOW TO DO IT

1. Cut an arm's length of string.
2. Hold the end of the string in your left hand.

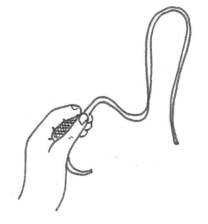

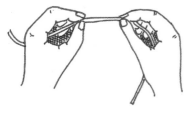

COLLECT TOGETHER

From nature:

A stick

String

3. Pinch the string with your right hand, slide it along the string a finger's length, and twist into a loop (this is the pinch-slide-twist). You have now made your fish, and the fish's tail should bounce with your right hand.

4. Pinch the fish's tail quickly before it swims away.

5. Pinch-slide-twist to the right of your fish to create the dish in just the same way.

6. Holding both your fish and your dish, put your fish on the dish by folding the loops together, slip both on to your stick and pull tight.

7. You have now created your fish on a dish knot. Really well done!

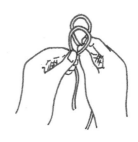

Lashing

Lashing is a skill that Outpackers use all the time when they're creating in the outdoors. It's used to secure sticks together in a really strong way. Once you've learned how to lash properly, you'll be able to make a raft fit for the rapids, a bat fit for any bat-and-ball game, and a multi-coloured super trampoline fit for any over-worked fairy. And that's even before you start to think of all the fantastic things that you can invent once you can lash two sticks together.

COLLECT TOGETHER

From nature:
Sticks

From the Out Pack
String
Scissors

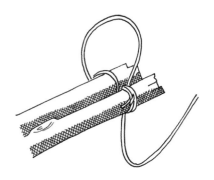

HOW TO DO IT

1. Place the sticks you wish to lash next to each other.

2. First, tie your fantastic fish-on-a-dish knot onto the end of one of your sticks.

3. Take your string and weave it under and over your sticks – however many you wish to lash. This will fasten them together. Do this lots of times, leaving an arm's length of string to tighten them.

4. Tighten the string in between the sticks by winding the tail end of the string around the join. Secure with a knot. A granny knot is fine (See step 5). The fish-on-a-dish knot is hard to use when you're tying the end of the string.

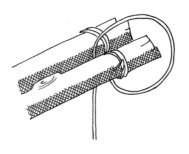

5. A granny knot is when you tie one end of string to another end of string. Simply cross the two ends, pass one end under the other and pull tight. To complete the knot, cross the ends again and pass one under the other. Pull tight and this knot should hold.

6. Now get thinking – what else can you make now that you can lash sticks together?

Den Building

This skill teaches you how to build your own den, out in nature and out of nature. Imagine you need to sleep out in the woods and you need to make your own shelter. Or more likely that you're having a picnic in the woods with your mum or dad and you'd like to build a den.

All you'll need from your Out Pack is string. The rest of your den will come from whatever is lying around on the ground.

This particular den is made just the right size for you: from your head down to your toes.

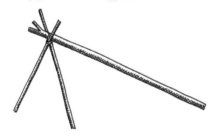

WHERE CAN YOU MAKE YOUR DEN?

Find an area that has lots of materials around like branches, sticks and leaves, so that you don't have to carry them far.

HOW TO DO IT:

1. Find a strong stick that's a head longer than you. This is your tall stick.

2. Now find two sticks that come up to your chin.

3. Lie your three sticks on the ground next to each other, with your tall stick in the middle. Take a two-arm's length of string and tie a good knot around the end of the three sticks.

Remember,

If it's made by nature, it can stay.

If it's from the Out Pack, take it away.

Wrap more string around and around the sticks and secure with another good knot.

4. Lift the chin-height sticks to make a triangle shape. This makes the frame for your den.

5. Collect lots of sticks of different heights and rest them against the tall stick all the way along on both sides. Make sure there aren't too many big gaps.

6. Now collect fallen leaves, grass, bracken, leaf litter, pine needles, broken leafy branches, small sticks – anything you can find. Starting at the bottom, cover the walls of your den and work your way to the top. If there is a lot of leaf litter around the base of your shelter, try to scoop it up the sides.

7. You can make a bed if you want to with soft, dry materials such as fallen leaves and grass.

8. If you'd like a bigger den, so that more people can fit inside, make your chin sticks higher. Sleep well!

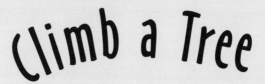

Climb a Tree

Climbing trees is a lot of fun. When you find a good, strong tree with lots of low branches, and you know all the special rules about how to climb safely, you'll be like a nimble little mountain goat. Skilfully moving from one branch to another, able to see for miles and always out of harm's way.

Tree-climbing Rules

- If you're sure that today is a good day for tree climbing, have a think about what you're wearing. Most important are your shoes. Pumps, trainers and well-fitting wellies are fine. Flip-flops are not! Also, are you dressed as a pirate or princess? Although pirates and princesses are extremely good at tree climbing, they do need to wear sensible clothes for the job. Make sure that your clothing doesn't have any bits that might get stuck on branches and take off your scarf.

- Be sure to find a tree with low branches.

- Do a wobble test to make sure your tree is safe to climb. If your tree or branch is rotten, it will really wobble. If it does, don't climb this tree. Also look around the trunk of the tree and keep an eye out for black, rotten wood.

- If the tree is wet, don't climb it.

- Take a moment to check out your tree and think about where you might put your feet and hands as you climb. This is called visualisation and is a skill in itself. It's more helpful than you might think!

- Once you have started climbing, make sure that you have always got three parts of your body in contact with the tree. This means two hands and one foot or two feet and one hand holding on to the tree.

- Only climb on branches that are thicker than your arm, and carefully do a little wobble test before you put all your weight on them.

- After each move, look down to check how high you've climbed. It's easier to climb up than down.

- On your way down, retrace your route.

- Oh and don't ever forget ... have fun!

Remember, always three on the tree!

Plaiting

This is a simple and decorative way of putting wool, coloured string or even willow together to make your creations look super cool. A dragon's harness, a fairy stepladder, your caterbling and butterbling ... whatever you like.

HOW TO DO IT:

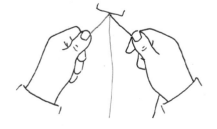

1. Take three pieces of wool or string of the same length.

2. Tie the ends together in a knot and stick it to the floor, a log or your Out Pack with a piece of masking tape.

3. Fan out the pieces of wool or string and take the two outside pieces in each of your hands.

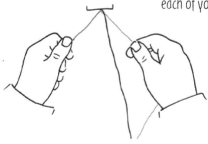

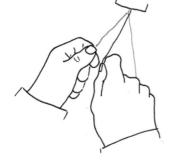

YOU WILL NEED

From nature:
Anything you can plait: string, wool, willow

From the Out Pack
Masking tape

4. Bring one of the outside pieces into the middle and fan again. Then bring the outside piece from the other side over this one. At this point you will need to tighten the plait by holding all the pieces at the same time and pulling gently. You should see the plait growing underneath the knot.

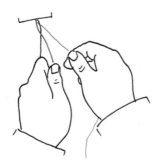

5. Continue doing this until you get the length of plait that you want. Then tie it off with a knot.

6. Go get that dragon harnessed up and head out for a flight ...

So you're an Outpacker

You now know great and wonderful things about the natural world around you. You know about seasons, the sky, about raft making, and how to make a fairy a relaxing place to hang out. This all makes you unbelievably special... This all makes you an Outpacker.

So, wherever you go... the park, the woods, your back yard or even the beach or the mountains, you can meet, make and imagine. You could make an Out Pack stay and play, an Out Pack weekend club or an Out Pack after-school club. There is plenty for you to do and enough nature to keep you all making and imagining.

Remember...

Coat, boots, Out Pack and go!

Other fun stuff to see and read

Parents, grandparents and teachers, have a look at **Project Wild Thing**. A fantastic film-lead movement to get more kids outside reconnecting with nature.

'This film will change your life'
Patrick Barkham, *The Guardian*.

The National Trusts' **50 Things to do Outdoors before you're 11 ¾.** A list of 50 more ideas of things to do outdoors.

Have a look at **The Nature Detectives** by The Woodland Trust (www.woodlandtrust.org.uk) and The Wildlife Trusts (www.wildlifetrusts.org). They always have an abundance of wonderful ideas for outdoor projects and activities in your local area.

Index

Ash 114
Animals 110–111
Autumn Out and
   Abouts 102–107

Beech 109
Birds 106–107
Blast Off 44–47
Bluebell 117
Bugs 112–113
Butterbling 28–29
Buttercup 123
Butterflies 118–119

Caterbling 26–27
Centipede 113
Cirrus 125
Classic Raft 30–31
Climb a Tree 136–137
Climbing Leaf 62
Clouds 124–125
Clove Hitch 130–131
Clover 123
Crab Apple 115
Croquet 76–77
Crow 106
Cumulonimbus 124
Cumulus 125

Den Building 134–135
Drum 52

Elder 121
Elf Garden 37
Enchanted Wings 24–25

Fairy Tree House 36
Fire-breathing Dragon
   48–49
Fish on a Dish Knot 130–131
Flowers 116–117, 122–123
Foraging 15
French Cricket 74–75
Fungi 104–105

Games 64–97
Games for One 92–97
Games Kit 68–69
Goose Grass 90
Guitar 51

Hit It, Bounce It 95
Hoopla 80–81
Horse Chestnut 103
How to keep score 67
How to pick who goes
   first? 67

Jackdaw 107
Jelly Ear 105

Lashing 132–133
Lesser Celandine 122
Lime 121

Magic 60–63
Magic Disappearing
   Stick 63
Magnetic Stick 60–61
Makey Games and
   Sticky Games 84–97
Memory Mobile 32–33
Millipede 113
Mouse 110–111
Mudasaurus 34–35
Mud Pie Market
   54–55

Nature Boules 72–73
Nature Makes 20–63
Neptune's Fishing
   Game 86–89
Nimbostratus 125

Oak Tree 102
Obstacle Course 82–83

Out and Abouts 98–125
Outpacker 17, 140

Painted Lady 119
Plaiting 138–139
Puddle Pictures 58–59
Puff Ball 105

Rabbit 110–111
Red Admiral 119
Rock Band 50–53
Rock Castanets 53
Rook 107
Rounders 78–79
Rowan 120

Scots Pine 109
Seasons 18
Season Star 42–43
Skills 126–139
Skip and Hop 96–97
Silver Birch 108
Small White 118
Snowdrop 116
Speedwell 117
Spring 114–119
Squirrel 110–111
Sticky Bud Tales 90–91

Sticky Spider Catch 92–94
Summer 120–125
Sweet Shop Scales 56–57
Sycamore 103

The Out Pack 13, 14
Trees 102–103, 108–109,
    114–115, 120–121
Turkey Tail 104

Weeping Willow 114
Winter 108–113
Wobble Catch 70–71
Wonky Racer 38–41
Woodlouse 112

Acknowledgements

Thanks to Izzy and Ben for trying out all our ideas with unquenchable enthusiasm. To Colin, Pam, and Victoria Webb for your invaluable advice. To Allan and Dawn at Copywrite for making something with our work that people took seriously and to Laura Long for reading it with such detailed attention. Thanks to Michael Palin and Helen Meech for their kind words and to David Bond for starting our book so perfectly. Thanks to Pavilion Books for taking us on this journey.

Steph would also like to thank her mum, dad and husband Pete for always helping with everything and for rarely questioning why. Thank you to Katie for coming up with the idea in the first place. And one final thank you goes to James, for the magic and because you above everyone else would have known what all this means.

Katie would also like to thank her amazingly supportive family, especially Matt for giving her space and time to make it happen. She would also like to thank Archimedes Forest School Education for teaching her the 'fish-on-a-dish' knot and for opening her eyes to the true wonders of outdoor education.